EYEWITNESS
EXPLORERS

Human Body

Written by
STEVE PARKER

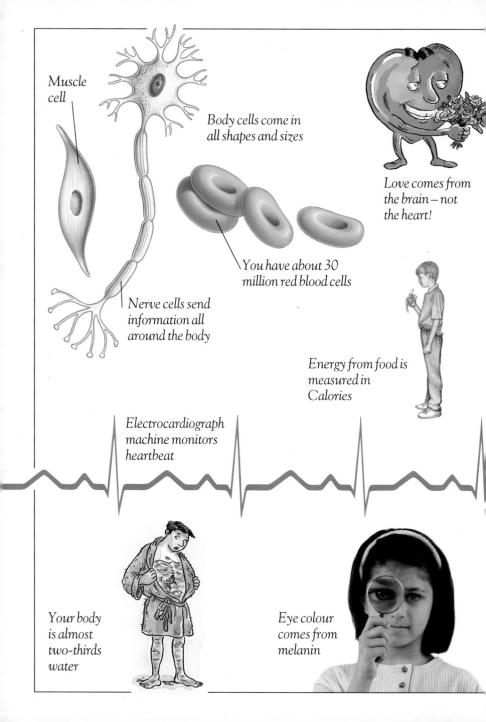

Muscle cell

Body cells come in all shapes and sizes

Love comes from the brain – not the heart!

You have about 30 million red blood cells

Nerve cells send information all around the body

Energy from food is measured in Calories

Electrocardiograph machine monitors heartbeat

Your body is almost two-thirds water

Eye colour comes from melanin

EYEWITNESS
EXPLORERS

Human Body

Written by
STEVE PARKER

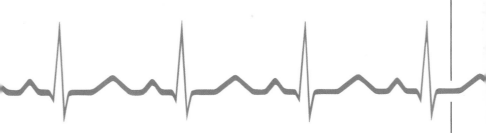

DORLING KINDERSLEY
London · New York · Stuttgart

A DORLING KINDERSLEY BOOK

Editor Djinn von Noorden
Art Editor Tina Robinson
Project Editor Mary Ling **Production** Catherine Semark
Editorial consultant Dr. Sarah Brewer

This Eyewitness ® Explorers book
first published in Great Britain in 1994 by
Dorling Kindersley Limited
9 Henrietta Street
Covent Garden
London WC2E 8PS

A CIP catalogue for this book is available from the British Library.

ISBN 07513 6101 1

Colour reproduction by Colourscan, Singapore
Printed in Spain by Artes Gráficas Toledo, S.A.
D.L.TO: 853-1996

Anatomical models supplied by Somso Modelle, Coburg, Germany
Visit us on the World Wide Web at
http://www.dk.com

Contents

Looking at your body

How many machines can do all the things that a human body can do? The body can run and jump, work out sums, feed and mend itself, laugh and cry. Exploring the body is fascinating. It's easy too – everybody has one!

Get to know yourself

Your body is so interesting, it's hard to know where to start. Why not begin with skin? Look at your hand under a magnifying glass. Is all the skin the same?

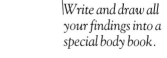

Skin on finger's has tiny creases

Write and draw all your findings into a special body book.

Skin underneath is paler than skin on top

Some bodies are tall, others are short.

Skin comes in lots of colours.

Shapes and sizes

Why does everyone look different? Even children of the same age come in all shapes and sizes. Details make us the way we are – hair and skin colour, shapes of noses and lips, and how we walk and talk.

Body origins

Most scientists agree that the human body has evolved (changed) over millions of years, from an ancient monkey-like creature. They have found very old bones that show how the changes happened.

Inside view

You know what your friends look like from the outside. But do you know what they look like inside? Make a body map and find out! You'll need a friend, a large sheet of paper, and some coloured pens.

✋ *Ask permission before you stick anything to the wall!*

1 Put a large piece of paper on the floor or fix it to the wall. Get your friend to lie on the paper as you draw around her body.

2 Now add the heart, lungs, and stomach. Check in the book to see if you were right. Are the body parts where you thought they would be?

Tight clothes help you see the outlines.

Some bodies are wide, others are slim.

Babies have large heads compared to their small bodies.

What am I?

Have you ever looked in the mirror and wondered what's under your skin? Organs! Skin, the muscles underneath, your heart, lungs, and brain are all organs. Every organ is made from millions of tiny living parts, called cells.

Robo-child
Imagine your body as a robot, made from lots of mechanical parts. Each part does one job to keep the robot working.

Brain works like a computer

Lungs work like bellows to suck in and push out air

Stomach works like a food mixer to mash up your meals

Body systems
Your body has dozens of organs, all working together to make a breathing, moving, feeling person. Groups of organs working together to do one job are called a system – like your digestive or nervous systems.

Leg bones work like stilts to hold up body

A tight fit

About ten of your main organs are packed inside your torso (central body). The top part of your torso contains your heart and lungs. The lower part contains several systems including your digestive system – your stomach, liver and intestines.

Blood vessels carry blood around body

Right lung

Liver processes digested food

Small intestine takes in nutrients from food

Lungs take oxygen from the air

Heart

Stomach holds food and drink from meals

Large intestine deals with left-over wastes from food

Doughnut-shaped red blood cells carry oxygen around the body.

Cell selection

The cells that make up your organs are so small that over 200 of them could fit onto this full stop. There are many kinds of cells, each designed to do a special job.

Long nerve cells send messages from one part of the body to another.

Spindle-shaped muscle cells contract (get shorter) to move the body.

Splish, splosh

The human body is about two-thirds water. This is mostly inside cells and in liquid parts such as blood. Even bones, which are hard, are one-third water.

What can I do?

Even the simplest actions aren't as straightforward as you think. Walk along. Your hips and knees bend; your feet lift up; your arms swing to balance – your body does all this just to walk a few steps! Timing lots of movements in the right order like this is called coordination.

Body action
It would be difficult to program a robot to make a human wheelbarrow shape. Yet when you do it, you don't even think about it.

Underwater world
An underwater swim? No problem! You can open your eyes underwater. And unless you turn upside-down, the air in your body stops water from getting into your nose and mouth.

Hand muscles keep fingers gripping

Hip and leg muscles hold legs out straight

Neck and shoulder muscles bend neck so head looks forward

Knees lock legs straight, to support extra weight of partner

Elbows keep arms straight to support body weight

Head senses swaying movements and keeps body balanced

Feet and toes keep body stable

Wrists are strong and flexible

Pat, rub

Pat your head with one hand. Rub your tummy with the other hand. Now do both together. Is it difficult? Think hard, and keep trying – your coordination will improve with practice.

Your brain helps you to coordinate the two movements.

Rub your tummy in small circles.

Stand, topple

Your body can't do everything. Stand with your left shoulder and foot pressed against a wall. Now try to lift the right foot – you won't be able to without falling over! To stand on one leg, your body needs to tilt, but the wall stops you.

Wriggle, wiggle

Your body can do things you don't even know about! Try wiggling your ears; everyone has ear-wiggling muscles, but most people don't know how to use them.

Try moving different muscles around the side of your head.

Backflips can be dangerous.

Practice makes perfect

Can you do handstands, somersaults, and backflips? With teaching and plenty of practice, most young people can. It's amazing what your body can do – if you really try.

A healthy body

You only have one body, and it has to last all your life – so look after it carefully!

Like a favourite pet, you need to keep it clean, feed it well, and make sure it gets lots of exercise and plenty of rest.

Brush your teeth after every meal.

Too tired!
If your body feels sleepy, it is for a good reason. Don't ignore it! People who try to stay awake too long get confused, suffer headaches, and cannot work or play at their best.

Keep clean
Every day, dirt and germs collect all over your body. Washing gets rid of germs, and prevents nasty smells. And don't forget to blow your nose, wash your ears, and cut your nails.

You lose the most heat from your head and upper body.

Keep comfortable
If you feel cold, you put on an extra jumper. When you're hot, you take it off. Clothes help your body to stay at its best working temperature by trapping a layer of air against the skin, which keeps in warmth.

Keep eating

Food is important for two reasons. It contains energy to power your muscles. It also helps the body to grow and maintain itself. But you can't just live on chocolate or sweets – as well as being bad for your teeth, your body won't work properly if it only gets one sort of food.

Brown bread contains starch, which gives you energy.

Try fruit in your lunchbox rather than chocolate or sweets.

Orange juice has plenty of vitamins.

Time for bed

Even though you might hate bedtime, your body doesn't. While you sleep, it carries on growing and repairing itself. Your body and brain never shut down at night – they just slow down. Most children sleep for about eleven hours every night.

You spend around a third of your life asleep!

Sensational skin

Skin does a lot more than simply keep your insides in. It protects the delicate parts beneath from knocks and bumps, keeps in body fluids, and keeps out harmful poisons. Your skin also helps to control temperature, and provides your sense of touch.

Sun
Skin contains a coloured substance called melanin, to protect you from the sun's ultraviolet rays. In light-skinned people, more melanin forms when they are out in the sun – this is a suntan.

All the colours under the sun
Skin can be white, pale pink, beige, cream, brown, or black. But everyone looks much the same underneath!

Light skin may burn in the sun.

Darker skin tans more easily than pale skin.

The darker the skin, the more melanin it contains.

Inside skin

The skin has two main layers. The outer layer is the epidermis. It is covered with tough, dead cells. Below is the dermis, which is packed with touch-detecting sensors. In real life, this skin would only be as thick as the line of this l.

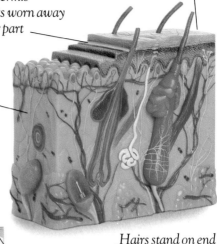

Tough upper epidermis protects delicate dermis

Lower epidermis replaces bits worn away from upper part

Dermis

Too hot or cold?

Skin helps to control body temperature. It loses heat when the body is too warm, and keeps it in when the body is cool.

Sweat cools skin as it dries

Hot
When you are hot, blood vessels widen to lose heat.

Hairs stand on end to trap air and retain heat

Cold
When you are cold, blood vessels narrow to keep in heat.

Fingerprints

The skin on your fingers is covered with a pattern of tiny ridges. Like the soles on a pair of trainers, they help you grip better. Each person's pattern is different – so no one else in the world has the same fingerprints as you.

These fingerprint patterns are called whorls.

17

Hair and nails

What do you have in common with a pet dog or cat? Fur and claws! As well as the hair on your head, tiny hairs grow all over your body. This hair is like an animal's furry coat, only much shorter and finer. Your nails also grow in the same way as an animal's claws, but in a different shape.

Hair grows here
Your hair grows from follicles (tiny pits) in the skin. Only the hair under the skin is alive. The hairs you see are rods of dead cells, hardened with a tough material called keratin.

Types of hair
Hair contains melanin – the same substance that colours skin. Hair colour depends on the amount of melanin in it. A little melanin makes fair hair, a lot makes darker hair.

Straight hair has a round follicle.

Curly hair has a flat follicle.

Hairy head

You have around 5 million hairs on your body – but only about 100,000 grow on your head. Head hair grows about 2 mm each week, and faster in summer than in winter. If you don't have your hair trimmed regularly, the ends become frizzy.

This hair has not been trimmed for a while. The end is split and uneven.

Hair needs to be at least 15 cm long

Hanging by a hair

The hair on your head is a lot stronger than it looks. Why not test how strong it really is? You will need a selection of friends' hairs, a small plastic bag, some marbles, and sticky tape.

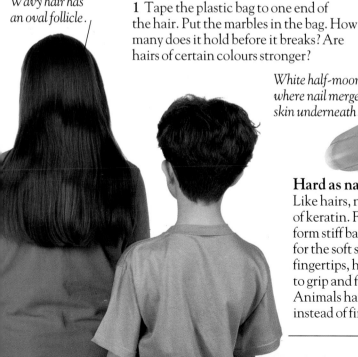

Wavy hair has an oval follicle.

1 Tape the plastic bag to one end of the hair. Put the marbles in the bag. How many does it hold before it breaks? Are hairs of certain colours stronger?

White half-moon shows where nail merges with skin underneath.

Hard as nails

Like hairs, nails are made of keratin. Fingernails form stiff backing pads for the soft skin of your fingertips, helping them to grip and feel pressure. Animals have claws instead of fingernails.

19

Muscles

Clench your fist. Can you see the muscles moving in your hand and wrist? You have over 600 strong, stretchy muscles all over your body. Every move you make is powered by muscles – from raising an eyebrow to running at full speed.

Your muscles
The biggest muscles are in your buttocks and thighs. The smallest, as thin as cotton thread, are inside your ear.

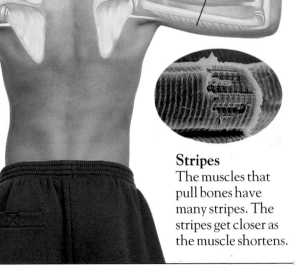

Biceps muscle pulls on upper forearm and bends elbow

Triceps muscle pulls on lower forearm to straighten elbow

Working in pairs
Most muscles pull on bones to make them move. A muscle only pulls. It cannot push, so muscles often work in pairs. Here, one muscle pulls to bend the elbow. The other muscle pulls the arm straight again.

Stripes
The muscles that pull bones have many stripes. The stripes get closer as the muscle shortens.

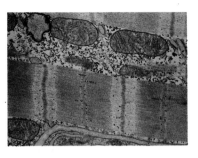

Non-stop muscle

Many of your organs are partly made of muscle, such as your heart, stomach, and intestines. Your heart muscle is called cardiac muscle. It never tires, and keeps your heart beating all your life.

Making faces

There are more than 40 muscles in your face. Some are joined to bones, such as your jaw. Some join to other muscles. There are circles of muscles in your eyelids and lips.

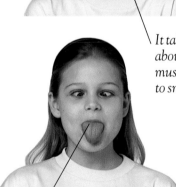

It takes about 10 muscles to smile.

It takes about 12 muscles to frown.

How many funny faces can you make?

Ouch!

Sometimes, muscles that have not been well used for a while become hard and tight. We call it a cramp. It is very painful! You can gently rub and stretch the muscle to make a cramp go away.

All about bones

Squeeze your arm. Can you feel the hard bone inside? Bones are the strong, stiff parts that support the soft body organs. They form a rigid frame inside your body, called the skeleton.

Floppy body
Your skeleton doesn't just hold your arms and legs straight. Without bones to anchor and protect your organs, your body would collapse in a heap.

Shoulder blade is broad and wide

Upper-arm bone is long and slim

27 bones in wrist and fingers

Ribs protect lungs

Bone in hip is called pelvis

Thigh bone is the biggest bone

Kneecap is small and round

Two bones in shin (lower leg)

26 bones in ankle and foot

The skeleton
There are 206 bones in the body, and they come in all shapes and sizes. Your thigh bone is long and thick, while the bones in the tips of your toes are tiny. Most of these bones are linked together at flexible joints so that you can move around easily.

Joined together
A bone meets another bone in a joint. Strong straps called ligaments hold the bones together so they can move, but not come apart.

Hip bone

Criss-cross ligaments in hip joint

Thigh bone

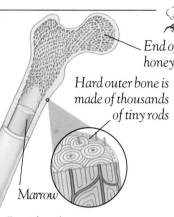

End of bone has honeycomb-like centre

Hard outer bone is made of thousands of tiny rods

Marrow

Skull bone protects brain inside

Inside a bone
Bones are not completely solid. In a long bone like the thigh bone, there is a space called the marrow cavity. It contains jelly-like marrow that makes new cells for the blood.

The spine
Your backbone is made of 33 small bones called vertebrae. They link to make a bendy tower. Cartilage is a strong rubbery material. Discs of cartilage sandwiched between the vertebrae stop them from grating together.

Skull is supported by atlas bone

Ring-shaped vertebrae protect the spinal cord inside

Cartilages allow spine to twist and bend

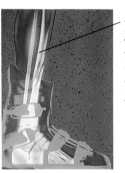

An X-ray picture shows the bones as white shapes.

Tailbone is lowest bone in spine

Baby bones
The bones of a newborn baby contain a lot of cartilage and its skull bones are not fused (joined) together. During the first two years of a baby's life, its skull bones fuse.

Break a leg
If you've ever broken a bone, you'll know how painful it is. If a doctor quickly sets the broken bone in plaster to keep it steady, it should mend and heal as good as new.

Soft part of baby skull is called the fontanelle

Heart

Put your fingers in your ears, shut your eyes, and listen. Can you hear your heart? A heart is a hollow lump of muscle as big as your clenched fist. Every second of your life, your heart pumps blood around your body.

From the brain
We say that emotions such as love come from the heart – in fact, they come from the brain.

A powerful pump
The left side of the heart pumps blood from the lungs to the rest of the body to give it oxygen. The right side pumps blood from the body back to the lungs for more oxygen.

Aorta carries blood to body's cells

High-oxygen blood returns from lungs to left pump

Low-oxygen blood returns from body to right pump

Right pump sends blood to lungs for more oxygen

Left pump sends high-oxygen blood around body

Open valve   Shut valve

One-way valves
Valves in the heart make sure the blood flows the correct way. Many larger veins also have valves. If blood tries to flow backwards, little flaps balloon out and seal together to prevent it doing this.

Heartbeats

The heart's blood-squeezing motion is called a heartbeat. You can hear it through a device called a stethoscope. To make one, you will need some rubber or plastic tubing, modelling clay, and two plastic funnels.

Move funnel around until beat is loudest

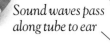

Sound waves pass along tube to ear

Funnel collects sound made by beating heart

1 Push a funnel into each end of the tubing. Secure with a·blob of modelling clay.

2 Hold one funnel to your ear and the other over a friend's chest, slightly to the left. Listen for the "lub-dup" sound of the valves snapping shut with each beat of the heart.

Feel your heart

The heart's powerful pumping sends a surge of blood around the body. You can feel this in your wrist, by placing two fingertips on the thumb side. It is called the pulse.

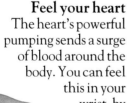

Use two fingers to feel towards the edge of your wrist.

Count the beat

The pulse rate is the number of beats in one minute – it is the same as the heartbeat rate. Here are some typical pulse rates. Measure your own when you are resting, and after some tiring exercise.

♥ ♥ ♥ ♥ ♥ ♥
Adult at rest 60-80

♥ ♥ ♥ ♥ ♥ ♥ ♥
Child at rest 90-100

♥ ♥ ♥ ♥ ♥ ♥ ♥ ♥
New baby at rest 120

♥ ♥ ♥ ♥ ♥ ♥ ♥ ♥ ♥ ♥
Adult after hard exercise 100-180

Blood

Next time you have a small cut or scrape, take a good look at your blood. This miracle liquid flows around your body like a river, bringing food and oxygen to all the cells. It spreads out warmth, and distributes chemicals called hormones. It also clots, to help seal and heal a wound.

Heart pumps blood around the body

Arteries carry blood away from the heart

See how it flows

Blood travels around the body in different blood vessels called arteries, capillaries, and veins. Each type of vessel is designed to do a different job.

Veins take blood back to the heart

Arteries divide and become smaller, until they are microscopic.

Tiny capillaries join to make veins

Green peaks

As the heart pumps, tiny electrical signals pass through it. An electrocardiograph (ECG) machine detects these and shows them on a screen.

Doctors look for a regular pattern

Blue blood

You can see some veins just under the skin. Rub your finger up a blue vein on the inside of your wrist; the blood will stop, then rush back through the vein when you let go.

The colour of the skin and vein wall makes the red blood inside look blue.

Blue veins show up best on light skin.

Look for a vein here

Put your finger here

Inside your blood

About half your blood is a pale yellow fluid called plasma, which contains sugars, salts, and hormones. The other half of your blood is made up of oxygen-carrying red cells, white cells, which fight infection, and clot-forming platelets.

From clot ...

If your skin or any other part of your body is damaged, the blood in the wound forms a sticky clot which seals the leak.

Platelets

Red cells

... to scab

The clot dries and hardens, forming a tough scab. This protects the skin underneath as it heals.

Blood chemicals make a net of fibres

Red blood cell

White blood cell

Scab forms protective covering

Edges of cut grow back together

Lungs and breathing

Nearly all living things, from worms to whales, need oxygen. You breathe in to supply your cells with oxygen – without it, they would die in a few minutes. Your cells also make a waste gas called carbon dioxide. Breathing out gets rid of this gas so that it does not poison the cells.

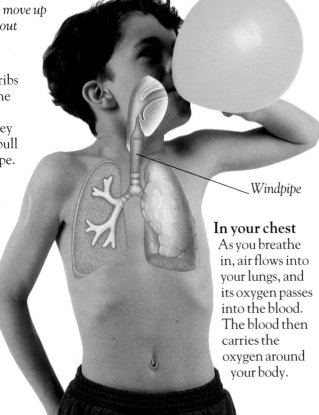

Air is sucked in

Ribs move up and out

Breathing in
To breathe in, your ribs move up and out. The muscle under your lungs flattens. As they expand, your lungs pull air into your windpipe.

Breathing out
To breathe out, your ribs move in. The muscle under your lungs bends up. Air squeezes out of the tiny air tubes in your lungs.

You have 300 million air pockets in each lung.

Windpipe

In your chest
As you breathe in, air flows into your lungs, and its oxygen passes into the blood. The blood then carries the oxygen around your body.

See your breath

On a cold day, you can see the air you breathe out. This is because your breath contains water vapour. As the water vapour meets cold air, it condenses into tiny droplets which look like puffs of white smoke.

Use a stopwatch to time your breaths.

Fast breaths

Most people breathe in about 10-20 times each minute. Try sitting quietly and counting your breaths for one minute. Now skip or jump for a while, then count your breaths for another minute. Are they faster? Busy muscles need more oxygen, so you have to breathe harder and faster to get it.

Breathing in, then out again, counts as one breath.

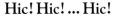

Hic! Hic! ... Hic!

Your diaphragm is the large muscle in the base of your chest that helps you to breathe. If it contracts more sharply than usual, your in-breaths come in gasps and make a "hic" noise. If you get a fright your hiccups might stop!

Food for life

All machines need fuel to make them go. Your body's fuel is the food you eat. Food gives you the energy to live and breathe, move and think, and keep warm. Food also contains nutrients, which your body needs to grow and repair itself.

Citrus fruits have vitamins for good health and fighting disease.

Wholegrain bread has lots of fibre.

Carbohydrates in bread, potatoes, pasta, and rice are a good source of energy.

Fibre in fresh fruit and vegetables keeps your digestion working well.

A balance of foods

Your body needs a variety of foods to stay healthy. There are three main groups of food; proteins, carbohydrates, and fats. Your body uses each group in a different way. As well as these, you need the fibre, vitamins, and minerals from fruit and vegetables.

Beans, fish, meat, eggs, and cheese contain proteins which are important for a growing body.

Cakes, chocolate, and cheese curls have lots of fat.

Fats store energy for the body to use – but don't eat too much of them.

Fruit juce is mostly water

Water to stay alive

Nothing can live without water. Your body needs two or three litres of water each day, which you get from foods as well as drinks.

Perfect food

A tiny baby cannot chew or digest solid foods. Its mother's milk provides it with a balanced mixture of nutrients. Mothers can choose to feed their babies with special milk from a bottle instead.

Babies get protein from mother's milk.

Eating energy

Food energy is measured in kJ (kilojoules) or Calories. A 10-year-old child needs about 2,000-3,000 Calories each day. Look on food packets to see how much energy the foods inside contain.

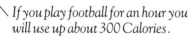

If you play football for an hour you will use up about 300 Calories.

What goes in . . .

The body makes two types of waste. Parts of your food that are too hard to digest pass out as solid waste. Your kidneys filter wastes from your blood and make urine, a liquid waste.

Teeth

Think what you would do without teeth. Food would be much less interesting. You would only be able to drink soup through a straw! Teeth bite and cut, chew and crush. They also help to shape sounds as you speak.

Stop the rot!
Sugary foods can harm teeth. Try leaving an old tooth overnight in a glass of cola. Is it any different in the morning?

Inside a tooth
A tooth has two main parts. The crown is the part above the gum. It is covered with enamel, which is the hardest substance in your entire body. The root is the part below the gum. It is fixed firmly into the jawbone.

Crown is part of tooth you can see

Enamel forms hard outer casing

Blood vessels bring nourishment to tooth

Dentine absorbs jolts and pressure

Cement

Jawbone

Last a lifetime
Teeth which are properly looked after can last dozens of years. If you keep your teeth clean and healthy, they will be something to smile about!

Types of teeth

There are 32 teeth in a full adult set, and four types of teeth. Each does a certain job. Chisel-shaped incisors cut and slice. Pointed canines spear and tear. The lumpy cheek teeth are premolars and molars, which crush and grind.

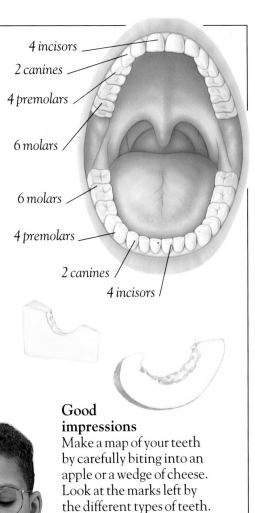

4 incisors
2 canines
4 premolars
6 molars

6 molars
4 premolars
2 canines
4 incisors

Two tooth sets

Babies are usually born without teeth, and grow 20 milk teeth by the time they are about three. At about six, the adult teeth begin to push out the milk teeth.

Mouth-watering

Your teeth wouldn't mash up food properly without saliva. Hold a cracker in your mouth – it soon turns soggy. This is because saliva makes dry foods moist and easier to chew and swallow.

Good impressions

Make a map of your teeth by carefully biting into an apple or a wedge of cheese. Look at the marks left by the different types of teeth. Are your teeth maps similar to those of your friends?

You make extra saliva (spit) when you chew and eat.

What happens to food?

When you swallow food, it starts a long journey through your body. As it travels through you, special chemicals break the food into particles which are small enough to be absorbed into your blood – this is called digestion.

Tall tubes

If your digestive tubes were pulled out, they would be 7 or 8 metres long. That's about five times longer than you are tall!

Where food goes

Food moves down your gullet into the stomach. It is mashed up, then squeezed along your intestines. The now-digested food particles pass from your small intestine into the blood, which takes them around your body.

Stomach slime

Your stomach has a slimy lining. This stops the strong chemicals from digesting the stomach as well as the food inside it.

Mucus-covered inner lining

Stomach has several thick muscle layers

Chewed food is pushed down gullet

Stomach

Liver processes digested food

Food is absorbed in small intestine

Waste food passes into large intestine and out through anus.

Body blender

Watch an adult putting different foods into a blender or processor. The machine cuts and mashes them into a thick soup, just like your teeth and stomach do. Like a blender, whatever you put into your mouth all looks much the same afterwards.

These fruits all have different colours and textures.

After blending or digestion, the fruit is reduced to a soupy pulp.

Tummy noises

Next time your stomach rumbles, try not to be embarrassed! It's only your digestive system squeezing and churning gas and digestive juices.

Eating upside down can make you choke!

Pushing food

Food doesn't just fall through your body. Muscles in the digestive tubes push it along, like toothpaste squeezing through a tube. That's why you can swallow even when you are upside down.

Neck muscles

Next time you take a bite of food, see if you can feel the muscles in your neck bulging as you swallow.

Food is pressed into ball that is easy to swallow

Gullet

Windpipe

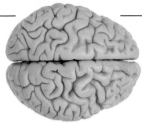

Amazing brain

Your brain is like a huge computer, controlling everything your body does. It governs your nervous system, as well as all your thoughts, feelings, and memories. Your brain looks like a large grey walnut. It fits snugly into the top part of your skull.

Two halves
The main part of your brain is in two halves, called hemispheres. Because the nerves to it cross over, each half of your brain controls the other half of your body.

Nerves in grey matter send messages to body

Ventricles are filled with fluid

Hunger and temperature control

Cerebral cortex

Cerebellum

Brain stem

Inside the brain
Parts of the brain do different jobs. Your cerebral cortex is the thinking area. Your cerebellum controls your muscles and balance. Your brain stem controls automatic actions, such as breathing.

Folded-up brain
Compared to other animals, you have a big brain for your body. The grey part of your brain is folded to fit inside your skull. Flattened out, it would cover an ironing board!

Sleepy head

Sleep is important for your brain – it needs to recover from the day's mental exercise. At night, your brain goes through 90-minute cycles of deep and shallow sleep. In deep sleep, it is relaxed; in shallow sleep, it is more alert.

You can have up to five or six dreams a night.

The thinking brain

Different areas of the cortex are in charge of various things. Some receive messages from your sense organs; others send messages to your muscles. The cortex also stores some information as memory. Close the book – then see if you can remember what the children are doing!

Motor centre controls muscles.

Touch centre receives nerve messages from skin.

Taste centre receives nerve messages from tongue.

Visual centre receives nerve messages from eyes.

Auditory centre receives nerve messages from ears.

Network of nerves

About 75 kilometres of nerves snake
through your body. Like a network of telephone
wires, they relay messages between your brain,
spinal cord, and body. The messages are in
the form of tiny electrical signals.

Axon

*Second
nerve
cell
body*

Signal down the line

A nerve cell communicates with lots of other nerve
cells through their dendrites. Nerve signals pass down
the dendrites, jump the tiny gaps to the nerve cell
body, and pass along its axon to other nerve cells.

Dendrite

*Signals have to jump across
tiny gaps called synapses*

*Axon of
first nerve*

Automatic action

If you prick your
finger, your hand
jerks back. This
reaction is called a
reflex. To do it as fast
as possible, the nerve
signals bypass your
brain and go directly
via your spinal cord
to the muscles.

*First nerve
cell body*

*Sensor
in skin*

*Skin on your fingertip
feels a sharp thorn*

*Nerve signals pass up
sensory nerve in arm*

Arm muscles jerk the hand away

Inside a nerve cell

A nerve cell has a control centre called a nucleus, just like other cells in your body. This nerve cell has several branches pointing away from the cell. The long thin axon takes a message out of the cell. The smaller, branching dendrites bring information into the cell.

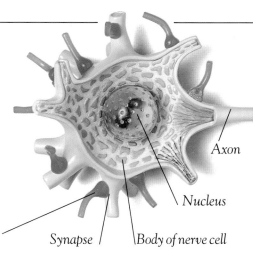

Axon

Nucleus

Dendrites from other nerve cells

Synapse

Body of nerve cell

Baby foot reflex

If you run your finger along a tiny baby's foot, it will curl its toes downwards. This reflex disappears as the baby gets older.

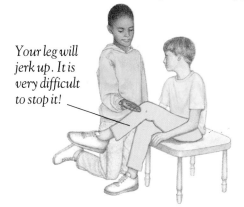

Doctors always test this reflex on newborn babies.

Pins and needles

If you cross your legs for too long, you may feel them tingle. When a nerve is squashed it can't work properly – the nerve sends signals, warning you to move.

Your leg will jerk up. It is very difficult to stop it!

Testing reflexes

Doctors use a special test to check if your nerves are working. Try it yourself! Sit on a chair with one leg crossed loosely over the other. Get a friend to tap your crossed leg just below the kneecap. What happens?

Hormones

Have you noticed how your heart thumps when you are scared? It's your endocrine system at work! Special organs called glands release hormones into your blood. Like tiny messengers, these hormones carry signals to the other organs all over your body.

Pituitary gland controls other glands

Thyroid gland

Adrenal glands speed up heart

Pancreas makes insulin

Ovaries control sexual development in girls

How hormones work

You have lots of endocrine glands. They all make different hormones. Each hormone affects other body parts. For example adrenaline, from the adrenal glands, makes your heart thump and gets you ready for action in an emergency.

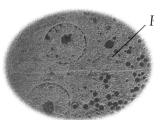

Pancreas cells under a microscope

Hormone-makers

Cells in your pancreas make a hormone called insulin. Insulin controls the level of sugar in your blood. In some people the cells do not work properly, and cause a condition called diabetes.

Waste disposal

Your kidneys filter out waste chemicals in your blood. They make urine, which you get rid of when you go to the toilet. A special hormone from the pituitary gland controls the amount of liquid your kidneys make.

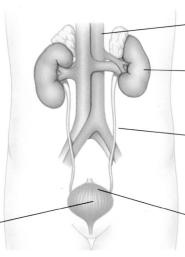

Blood flows into kidneys

Kidneys filter wastes from blood

Tubes carry urine from kidneys to bladder

Your bladder can expand to hold more than a cup of urine!

Bladder stores urine

Growing up

As a boy grows up, his testes (male glands) make more of the hormone testosterone. In addition to controlling the production of sperm cells, it makes hair thicken and grow, especially on his lower face.

A man has thicker facial hairs

A young boy has very fine hair on his face.

Fighting disease

Your thymus gland is just in front of your heart. It is important in fighting disease, because it trains white blood cells to recognize and help attack invading germs. Your thymus is especially active while you are young – as you grow older, it becomes less important.

Fighting fit

All around you are tiny germs, which are far too small to see. They float in the air, lurk on food, and even live on your skin. So how do you stay healthy? You are protected by an army of germ-fighting cells in your blood and lymph system.

Lymph
The main germ-fighting cells are white blood cells. They live in lymph, a fluid that flows around a network of lymph tubes and glands.

Coughs and sneezes
When you have a cough or cold, each time you cough or sneeze you blow out millions of tiny germs. These can be breathed in by other people. This is how illnesses are passed on.

Make sure you catch the germs in a handkerchief!

Invisible invaders
These tiny germs are called bacteria. Different bacteria cause illnesses such as sore throats and tonsillitis. Viruses are even smaller germs; they give you colds, chickenpox, measles, and many other illnesses.

Eating germs

One of the easiest ways for germs to get into the body is if you eat them. Acids and other chemicals in your stomach usually kill them – but sometimes there are just too many. The germs multiply in your intestines, causing illnesses such as food poisoning.

Sharing food passes germs from mouth to mouth.

Handy germs

Many of the things you touch every day have germs on them. By licking your fingers you could swallow the germs. So wash your hands regularly, especially before you eat.

Soapy water helps to remove and destroy dirt and germs.

Food hygiene

Make sure you cover or refrigerate food to protect it from pests. Flies and other insects spread germs – a fly walking on your dinner may have been running about on dog mess. And to soften their food before sucking it up, flies vomit onto it!

Communication

We communicate with each other by the sounds of speech, and by the silent signs of body language. When you are with friends, try suddenly looking very surprised, and pointing into the distance. Your friends may well look too! This is the power of sign and gesture. Watch how people talk, and use facial expressions, hand movements, and body positions.

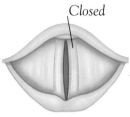

Open

Closed

Vocal cords
These two flaps are at the top of your windpipe. As air flows past them, they vibrate and make sounds.

Hold on, wait, OK ...
When you play games, you make signs and gestures with your face, arms, and hands. You learn these at an early age, and use them to tell others what you mean and want.

Raised eyebrows can mean surprise.

Try playing cat's cradle or other games without talking – does it make communication more difficult?

Use a piece of string or wool for cat's cradle.

I   love   you

Each sign means a word or a letter. These hands are saying "I love you!"

Sign language

People who cannot talk use a special sign language to communicate. Try out the signs above, and see if you can teach your friends to understand what you are saying.

Shadow person

Can you find this person in the book? You probably know the body language, just from the shape. It's amazing what your brain remembers for you!

Arm around shoulder shows concern and sympathy

Hiding face shows sadness

Smiling face shows happiness

Silent messages

Often you can show your feelings with no words at all. If you cover your mouth and look in a mirror, your eyes can still "smile". We rely on body language to understand each other. Can you guess the moods of these children? The boy playing soccer keeps his eye on the ball.

Eyes and sight

Of all the sense organs, your eyes receive the most information about the world around you. They can see shapes and colours, brightness and shadows. Try closing your eyes and finding your way around your home. Now you can "see" how much you rely on your eyesight.

Eye colour

Look at your eyes in a mirror. What colour are they? Eye colour is not the whole eye. It is only the colour of the eye's ring of muscle, the iris.

How you see

Light rays shine in through the cornea. The lens focuses (bends) the rays. They pass through the eyeball and shine on the retina. The retina turns the pattern of light rays into nerve signals which go to the brain.

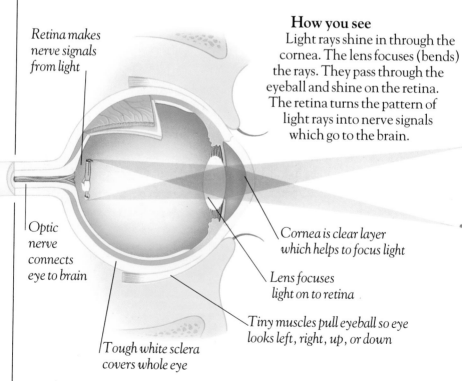

Retina makes nerve signals from light

Optic nerve connects eye to brain

Cornea is clear layer which helps to focus light

Lens focuses light on to retina

Tiny muscles pull eyeball so eye looks left, right, up, or down

Tough white sclera covers whole eye

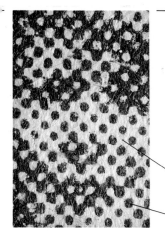

Join the dots

Look at a photograph in a newspaper. The shades of grey look smooth. Now look very closely with a magnifying lens – the photo is made of tiny black ink dots. If your eye cannot see the details, it "joins the dots" to make a solid colour. The pictures in this book are the same, made from ink dots in four colours.

White areas have hardly any black ink dots.

Black areas may be almost solid black ink.

See for yourself

One of your eyes is in charge of the other. This is your dominant eye. Find yours by holding one finger up in line with a distant object. Now cover each eye in turn, then uncover it again. When one of your eyes is covered, your finger seems to jump! The eye you are covering when this happens is your dominant eye.

Line your finger up with a friend or tree in the distance.

Your dominant eye helps you to judge angles and distances.

Lens defects

Short-sighted people cannot see distant things clearly. Long-sighted people see close objects as blurred. This happens when the eyeball is too big or too small for the focus of its lens. Spectacles or contact lenses correct the problem.

Short sight

Lens focuses image in front of retina

Long sight

Lens focuses image behind retina

Ears and hearing

Close your eyes, and ask a friend to clap nearby. Can you tell where your friend is from the direction of the clap? As well as sensing where sounds come from, your ears can hear a huge range of them, from deep boomy notes to high squeals, soft purrs to loud bangs, and nasty noises to beautiful music.

In a spin
Your ears help you to spin fast without falling over. Special parts called the semicircular canals, deep in your ear, help you keep your balance.

Outer parts of ear are cup-shaped to collect sound

What are sounds?
Put a glass against a wall. Can you hear sounds from the next room? Sounds are vibrations. We hear these vibrations when they travel through the air. Your ears collect them as sound waves. But sound waves also travel well through some solids, such as walls and glass. These make the sound waves louder so you hear them more clearly.

Keep your ear close to the glass

Inside your ear

You can see only part of your ear. The rest, shown here, is inside your head. Your outer ear funnels sound waves into a small tunnel, called the ear canal. The waves travel along this to the inner ear. They become nerve signals and go to the brain.

Semicircular canal helps to control balance

Cochlea converts sound waves into nerve signals

Listening to yourself

When you talk or chew, your inner ear receives sound waves through the bones in your head as well as through the air. This is why you sound different when you hear yourself on tape.

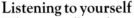

Use a tape recorder to record yourself playing an instrument.

Loud or soft?

Ears usually become less sensitive with age. What seems like a loud sound to a young person may be almost too quiet for some older people.

How loud is loud?

Your ears can pick up sounds as loud as a jet engine, and as quiet as a whisper. Scientists measure loudness in decibels (dB). Sounds above 90-100 dB are so loud that they can damage your ears.

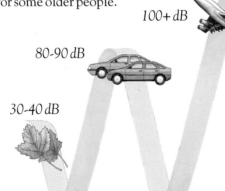

100+ dB

80-90 dB

30-40 dB

49

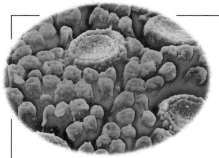

Tongue and taste

Can you remember the taste of your favourite food? And the food you hate the most? Your sense of taste comes from your tongue. It is covered with thousands of microscopic onion shaped sensors called taste buds. These detect the tastes and flavours in foods and drinks.

Tongue close-up
This is your tongue under a microscope. The little blue bumps form a rough surface which helps you chew food. The large pink bumps have taste buds on their sides.

Four flavours
You have thousands of taste buds concentrated along the tip, sides, and back of your tongue. Different areas of your tongue detect the basic flavours which are sweet, sour, bitter, and salty.

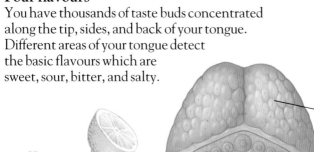

Coffee has a bitter taste which you sense on the back of your tongue.

You taste sour foods such as lemon juice with the middle sides of your tongue.

The sides of your tongue detect the salt in crisps and seafoods.

The tip of your tongue is sensitive to sugary foods.

Not just taste

Your tongue doesn't just taste. It is also a floppy muscle which helps to move food around in your mouth as you eat. It also moves very fast to make shapes for speaking. But that's not all! Along with sensors on the inside of your mouth, your tongue can feel whether food is hot or cold, lumpy or creamy, and dry or moist.

Sensors in your tongue warn you if food is too hot or cold.

🖐 *Hot drinks can burn you!*

Horrible taste

As we grow older, some of our taste buds die. A baby has over 10,000 taste buds; an old person has about 5,000. This is why some foods taste stronger to you than they do to grown-ups. So even if you don't like broccoli now, you may love it when you're older!

Working together

Your senses of taste and smell often work together. If you have a cold and cannot smell, you probably won't be able to taste food either. Strong smells can also confuse your taste buds. Why not try a taste test? You'll need cubes of apple, potato, an onion slice, and a blindfold.

🖐 *Ask an adult to cut the cubes for you*

1 Blindfold a friend. Give him some apple and potato cubes. Can he taste them?

2 Now hold the onion slice under his nose. Let him eat an apple or potato cube. What can he taste now?

Nose and smell

What's your favourite smell? Baking bread? Or a bunch of roses? Your nose is a very sensitive organ. As well as helping you to breathe, it can detect tiny quantities of smells in the air, and identify them. Your sense of smell can even save your life, by warning you of stinking food that could poison you, or by helping you smell smoke from a fire.

Smelly baby
Within a few hours of being born, a mother knows her baby by its smell. You won't be able to smell her baby, but can you find it here?

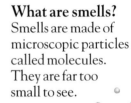

What are smells?
Smells are made of microscopic particles called molecules. They are far too small to see.

Smell molecules float from the perfume bottle into the air.

How you smell
When you breathe in, smells get sucked into your nose. They land on special hairy smell sensors inside. These detect the smells and send signals to your brain.

Rubbery nose

Try pressing your nose. It may feel bony, but it's made of pieces of rubbery cartilage. Muscles under the skin pull the cartilage so you can squash and wrinkle your nose.

Baby can smell its mother too!

Sniff the smell

Why do things smell stronger if you sniff them? Because when you breathe in, most of the air rushes past your smell sensors and down your throat. But when you sniff hard, you suck the air up near to the sensitive smell sensors.

Smell sensors are high up in nasal cavity

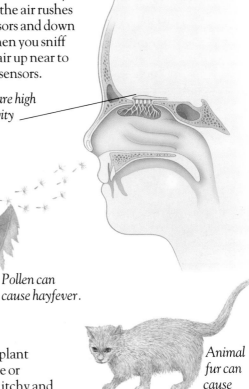

Feathers from pillows can cause allergies.

Pollen can cause hayfever.

Nose nasties

As well as smell molecules, many tiny things float in air, such as dust, fur, and plant pollen. Some people are sensitive or allergic to them. Their nose gets itchy and runny, and they sniff and sneeze.

Animal fur can cause allergies.

Touch

Your skin is the biggest touch organ in your body. You use it to sense an amazing amount about the world around you. These sensations come from millions of tiny sensors scattered throughout your skin. They tell you if your shoes rub, or if a fly lands on your face.

Helpful pain
Pain hurts, but it also helps. It warns you something is wrong, and tells you to move away.

Touch test
How much can you identify by touch? Try a touch test and find out! Start by cutting some hand-sized holes in a cardboard box.

Ask an adult to cut the holes for you.

Doing the test
Now put in things that feel funny, such as cold spaghetti, and peeled grapes. Ask your friends to feel what they are through the holes, without looking. Are their guesses always right?

Make the holes large enough for your hand.

Spaghetti feels slimy and slippery.

Grapes feel cold and wet.

Sugar feels soft and grainy.

Reading by touch

Fingertip skin is very sensitive. It can feel tiny lumps and bumps. Braille is a reading method for people who are blind or who cannot see clearly. The writing is printed as patterns of raised dots, which Braille readers feel with their fingers.

This is the alphabet written in Braille.

Feeling nothing

When skin is pressed for a long time by things such as socks, a belt, or a wristwatch, it loses its sensitivity. You can hardly feel them. That is, until you take them off, and see the squashed imprints they leave!

How warm is cold?

If you have been touching something cold, and then touch an object that is at normal temperature, it feels warm by comparison. Why not fool your temperature receptors with this experiment?

Don't touch the hot tap! Get an adult to help.

Hot   Warm   Cold

1 Fill three cups with ice water, hot water (but not so hot that it hurts to put your hand in), and warm water. Put a finger of each hand in the hot water and ice water for one minute.

2 Put both fingers in the warm water. How does the water feel on each finger? Now try the experiment again with two different fingers of *one* hand. What happens?

Hot   Warm   Cold

55

A new baby!

Did you know that you are nine months older than you think you are? This is because nine months before you were born, you started life as a tiny egg cell. The egg cell grew inside your mother. After nine months, the cell developed into a baby, ready to be born.

Big mother
The time a baby develops inside its mother is called pregnancy. The growing baby makes the mother's tummy bigger and bigger!

Getting together
A baby begins when a tadpole-shaped sperm cell from the father joins with an egg cell inside the mother. This is called fertilization. The egg splits in two, and then in four, and so on. It attaches itself to a part of the mother called the womb.

Inside the womb
The fertilized egg contains instructions to make a new baby, called genes. Everyone has two sets of genes, one from the father and one from the mother. Genes affect eye and hair colour, and many other features.

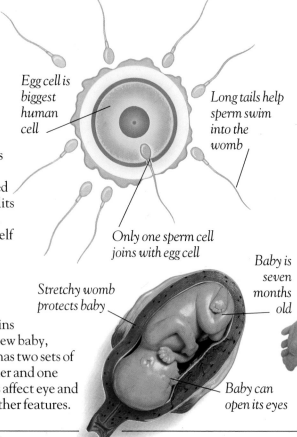

Egg cell is biggest human cell

Long tails help sperm swim into the womb

Only one sperm cell joins with egg cell

Stretchy womb protects baby

Baby is seven months old

Baby can open its eyes

Two in one

Sometimes a mother may have two babies at the same time, called twins. If the babies come from the same egg, they are identical – they look exactly the same.

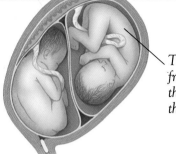

These twins are from two eggs – they won't look the same.

Baby's lifeline

A growing baby needs lots of nourishment. It gets this from its mother's blood, through a tube called the umbilical cord. When you were born, your cord shrivelled and dropped off. It left a small bump or hole which we call the navel or belly button.

Growing fast

A baby isn't as helpless as it looks. It has several reactions which help it survive. For example, it cries to tell its mother it wants food, drink, or a cuddle. Its fingers are strong. And the tiniest baby soon learns to recognize the smiles and voices around it.

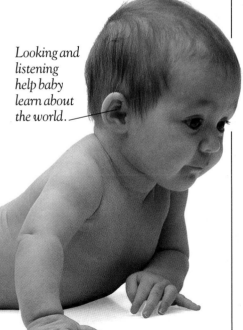

Looking and listening help baby learn about the world.

Legs kick to practise movements.

Growing up

Can you remember being small? You couldn't reach the light switch on the wall, and grown-ups looked so huge! Your body grows very fast during childhood, especially during the first two years. When you are about 11, your body changes again and you start to become an adult. This is called adolescence.

Older boy can work the yo-yo.

Learning about life
Growing up isn't just your body changing. Can you remember learning to walk? As you grow, you pick up skills and actions. There are always new things to learn, such as riding a bike or playing the piano!

Older girl can balance bricks to make a tower.

Baby learns to pick up bricks.

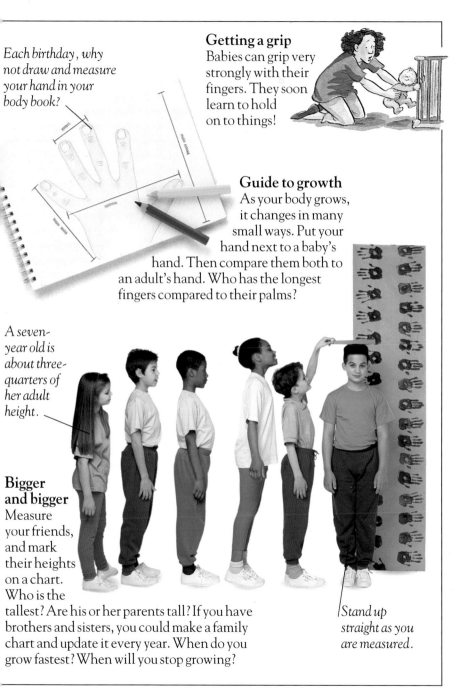

Each birthday, why not draw and measure your hand in your body book?

Getting a grip
Babies can grip very strongly with their fingers. They soon learn to hold on to things!

Guide to growth
As your body grows, it changes in many small ways. Put your hand next to a baby's hand. Then compare them both to an adult's hand. Who has the longest fingers compared to their palms?

A seven-year old is about three-quarters of her adult height.

Bigger and bigger
Measure your friends, and mark their heights on a chart. Who is the tallest? Are his or her parents tall? If you have brothers and sisters, you could make a family chart and update it every year. When do you grow fastest? When will you stop growing?

Stand up straight as you are measured.

59

Index

A

adolescence, 58
adrenaline, 40
allergies, 53
anus, 34
aorta, 24
arteries, 26
axon, 38, 39

BC

babies, 56-57
  head, 9
  bones, 23
  food, 31
  growing, 58-59
  reflexes, 39

Scab formation

smell, 52
teeth, 33
bacteria, 42
balance, 48
belly button, 57
bladder, 41
blood; 24, 26-27, 28
  cells, 11, 27, 42
  clots, 27
  vessels, 11, 17, 26
body language, 44, 45
bones, 22-23
Braille, 55
brain, 10, 36-37
breathing, 28-29

Calories, 31
capillaries, 26
carbohydrates, 30
carbon dioxide, 28

cartilage, 23, 53
cells, 11, 56
communication, 44-45
coordination, 12-13
cornea, 46
cramp, 21

Baby sniffing

DE

decibels, 49
dendrites, 38, 39
dermis, 17
diaphragm, 29
digestion, 34-35
dreams, 37

ears, 13, 37, 48-49
eating, 30-31
energy, 15, 30
epidermis, 17
eyes, 37, 46-47

Pulling faces

F

fats, 30
fibre, 30
fingerprints, 17
follicles, 18
fontanelle, 23
food, 15, 30-31, 34-35

G

genes, 56
germs, 14, 41, 42-43
glands, 40-41
growing up, 58-59
gullet, 34
gum, 32

Hair strength

HI

hair, 18-19
headache, 14
health, 14-15
hearing, 37, 48-49
heart, 11, 21, 24-25, 26
hiccups, 29
hormones, 26, 40-41
hygiene, 43

insulin, 40
intestines, 11, 34, 43
iris, 46

JKL

jawbone, 32
joints, 22

keratin, 18, 19
kidneys, 31, 41

legs, 10
ligaments, 22
liver, 11, 34
lungs, 10, 11, 28-29
lymph, 42

M

marrow, 23
melanin, 16, 18
milk, 31
minerals, 30
muscles, 11, 12-13, 20-21, 35, 38

N

OP

RS

Taste buds

Adult teeth

TU

VW

Acknowledgments

Dorling Kindersley would like to thank:

Iona Stevenson and the children of St. Mary Abbots School, Kensington, London especially Daniel Andrew, Dean Atta, Mimi Berchie, Francisco Jimenez-Rands, Terri Jones, Myles Morson, Alison Owen, Mariam Sheikh, Damaris Taylor, Jessica Whiteman, Snezana and Sasa Zivojinovic.
Darren Colyer and Gemma Ching-a-Sue for additional modelling.
Mark Haygarth and Susan St. Louis for design assistance.
Andy Crawford for photography.
Sharon Grant for help on the initial stages of the book.
Diana Morris for picture research.
Tammy Girl for children's clothes.

Illustrations by:
Julie Anderson, Michael Courtney, Nick Hall.

Picture credits
t=top b=bottom c=centre l=left r=right
Susanna Price: 31tr.
Science Photo Library: 27c, 42br; /Chris Bjornberg: 23c; /CNRI 19t, 20br, 40br; / Martin Dohrn 47t; /Don Fawcett 21t /Francis Leroy, Biocosmos 24c; /Omikron 50t.
Zefa: 12t.